Phases of an abstract mind

Alison Bonasoro

BookLeaf Publishing

India | USA | UK

Presentation by *BookLeaf Publishing*

Web: www.bookleafpub.com

E-mail: info@bookleafpub.com

ISBN: 9789357617185

First edition 2023

DEDICATION

I would like to dedicate this book to anyone who may need someone who gets it.

 Also to a few people who I couldn't have done this without.

 J-The first person who made me realize I had a voice.

 M-The first person who helped me realize I could and wanted to pursue my writing.

 M, S- The two who are always cheering me on and are always there and believing in me.

 K- The one who reads and never judges and always tells me to keep going.

ACKNOWLEDGEMENT

It took a lot of time. Going back and forth on whether I wanted to put myself in the world. I acknowledge that couldn't do this without the people who helped me realize I had a voice, never doubted I could do this, and who always read and never judged. Also, those who read these now.

PREFACE

I wrote these poems because I needed a way to express what I could never get out with spoken words. It's not always easy to verbalize what goes on upstairs. I only hope the words written in here, someone who needs to express what they are feeling can relate to these. That they know they aren't the only ones and someone understands.

A short Two Billion

Two billion miles apart yet so close to the naked
eye. Can't reach them,
can't touch them just floating among them.
So beautiful but just empty and held together by
its own gravity. We know how we want them to
appear; only the lucky ones get to see them for
real.
Two billion miles apart yet so close.

Silent guilt

I often wonder could he hear me?
If he could-
Did he smile when he heard my voice? Did he
know it was me? I wish I could recall the words
I said. I love you with all my heart, see you later.
The few fragments I remember.
Does he know I meant every word?
Would it make a difference if I was there? It's
not fair everyone that could see you did
It's not fair that I feel robbed of every chance
they all had
It's not fair, So I often wonder
Will I ever get to feel anything more than just
guilt And can I make it different for the next
time I have to go through this again?

Solitude

3

Ever since I was little, all I learned from the human race is that- there will always be someone else.

I got used to people choosing someone else over me and never being good enough for anyone. So why is it that I'm afraid to do things alone? You would think I would be okay with it by now. I guess I was never really alone, growing up in a huge family it's almost impossible to be alone entirely. Yet in the outside world it's rather simple; no matter how many people share your surroundings.

Two ends of hope

Can't.
Can't be hope,
Hopeful; hopeless
Can't have it.
All there is in this thread,
Hope ties;
Between me and all I want.
All I ever told myself what will be,
Is a dream.
Built on factual speculation.
Hope for you.

Footmark guide

It's okay, I know where I stand.
I may not know how I got here,
But I know where I stand.
My feet aren't planted together.
One stays behind me;
The other is my guide.
It's as if I don't know how to stand still,
My feet aren't planted together.
It helps me look back and look forward.

It's okay, I know where I stand.
I may not know how I got here.
But as long as my feet are never planted;
I'll know where I will be standing.
All because I knew where I stood.

Roots or petals

6

When is it okay to break a branch off a tree;
Especially when leaves still bud?
When is it okay to pick flowers straight from the
ground;
Especially when they don't need attending to?
If you know that it does more harm than good;
Why is it okay for others to take away the
beautiful parts of you?

A little lifetime

It doesn't matter!
If it was years ago or not.
You no longer think you moved past it.
They will make eye contact,
You're convinced they are doing that on
purpose.
To make you feel crazy;
As if they don't remember what they did.
Maybe they do-they probably do
You want to run away.
Yes as much as you want to,
You feel trapped.

You tell yourself,
Don't make eye contact.
Don't think of the brick in your stomach.
Keep telling yourself,
The hand you feel on your back isn't there.
Keep telling yourself,
It's just a little while.

I know it feels like a lifetime.
You know it was just a little while.
In the moment between the little while and the
lifetime;

You no longer think you moved past it.
By staying because you know there are greater
reasons too;
You moved past it!

More than light

You tell me to power through it,
But you don't know what "it" is.
I have been "powering" through it
For more than a year, for ten months and two
days, for as long as I can remember.
And sometimes, most times, for as long as I can
remember; I have been a flickering light.
A light bulb that isn't fully screwed in
A flashlight with batteries ran down
Or maybe I just haven't gotten much sun
Whatever it is, whenever I am fully connected to
my power source
It's the only light in the room; the only light you
need.
I can't promise it will always be that way.
Sometimes it will be flickering or even out
alltogether.
So don't tell me to "power through it"
Because maybe, just maybe
you need to be able to see in the dark.

Where to go from here

We're always told you can't have it both ways.
You can always standstill,
Keep moving forward or turn around. There's
North, south
East, and west.
Up, or down
Left, or right
Back and forth
Or side to side
Can't decide?
There's always an in-between.

12-18-21

If I could make it so,
I would forgive
What I'll never be able to forget.
All we have are memories.

Some would call it selfish
And I am one
It's a different kind of grief
And to not feel this
I hope they know how lucky they are.

Broken Thunder

If it is something you love
you'll make it work
The thunder cracked
The lightning struck
One more explosion
It was over
The power
The energy
The heat
Were nonexistent
Watching the storm
From the stairs
There was a clear view of the rain
The escape
The secret drought of day –
They could never make it work

Crickets

13

It's as clear as rain
It's as vivid as the first snowfall
It's as quiet as the night; just crickets
One more chance to hear or see it as real as life
I hear it in the songs I listen too
I look at the photos every day
But to talk too?
There're only crickets

Awareness

Don't think that a tree doesn't know when the
wind is too much
Don't think that the sea doesn't know how
strong the undertow is
Don't think that the stars don't know when they
aren't shining as much
Or that the sun doesn't know when it's not
breaking through an overcast
Just as you shouldn't think that I don't know as
well

Picture it

15

It's a warped puzzle isn't it?
All the pieces used to fit together.
Then one day, one piece got bent and jaded.
Their part of the picture started to peel off.
And suddenly the picture wasn't what it was
meant to be.
The piece can be forced to fit.
You can try to glue that part of the picture back
to its piece or even glue the entire puzzle
together.
Maybe even frame it so it has to stay the way
you saw it.
But you'll always know that, that one piece got
bent, jaded, and peeled.
Over all mended to be what you wanted it to be,
when fate had other intentions.

Shortcut fix

I need to know if you understand
That a broken bowl looks like it can hold your
soup, but it will still leak from underneath if it's
not reinforced long enough to be whole again.
There isn't any amount of tape or glue to seal the
cracks on their own.
Tape can peel off with time-
And glue won't stick on its own forever and
even if it seals; you can tell it was once broken

Always Knowing

I didn't know then
That I'd miss the time when
Every day you were there
I was the first to hold your hand
The first you ever met
As the days grew
You bickered, we argued
You sulked in silence
I kept a distance
I couldn't have known how much
You sculptured what I was to who I am
You showed my hands how to paint
While my feet learned to dance
You helped me grow crystals on a string
How to cast a line and create an electric one
You loved that I loved both ends
Weird and all
I never knew how important those moments
were
And now, I can't ask how you are

Super Nova

She sat on the Moon.
Fought her demons on Mars.
Got caught in her own red storm.
Skated on the rings of Saturn and swirled on the
surface of the first ice giant.
It was Neptune that gave her hope.
Although she was light years away, she found
herself dancing in the stars.

Losing a stranger

I don't know where you are, like I used to.
I don't know how you are, like I used to.
I'd go so far as to say I don't know you, like I
used to.
But I don't know you at all.

It's almost been a year
I don't remember the date of the last time I saw
you.
I don't remember the last thing I said in person.
It was almost Christmas and we ended up
arguing, in a group message.

I don't know you anymore
I don't know if I ever did
Because if I ever did
If I still do,
I wouldn't have to worry about losing you.

Maybe

20

I know you didn't mean anything by what you
asked.
It was just a question.
A simple question that I still think about.
I don't know if I ever was; I like to think as
such.
It all faded from view. It feels like another
lifetime ago
But I know now, that I want to be.
And if I ever was happy back then; I know I can
be again.

Only the beholder

How do you explain
Lyrics in a song,
Words in a book,
Paint on a canvas?
When it's possible
nothing is what it looks, sounds, or even feels
like.
When it's possible
Everything is what it looks, sounds, or even
feels like.
When the only truth lives in the mind; Becomes
real by the hands.
Only the creator can unveil it's masterpiece.

Phases

She always looked at the night sky
Felt connected in some way
The stars comforted her like a blanket Yet, it's
the moon she always hunted for
like a childhood stuffed animal she could never
sleep without As she grew older she didn't
always feel so connected to others And the
desire to star gaze and hunt for the moon was
still there but it slowly faded as she knew it was
human connection she really needed Always
amazed by its shapes And how it still shined the
same every night-even if she couldn't see it She
wondered how something so far away could
make a night shadow
"Why am I broken?" she thought-"the moon is
sometimes broken and people still look at it in
awe even when it's light years away." She could
always see the full moon even in its smallest
phase
"Just because something or someone doesn't
appear to be full doesn't mean it's empty or
broken" She finally knew why she felt
connected to the moon and comforted by the
stars She realized that even when she feels
broken-when she is in her smallest phase, she

shines fully for the ones that feel connected to
her.

23

www.ingramcontent.com/pod-product-compliance
Lightning Source LLC
Chambersburg PA
CBHW070730160726
48003CB00006BA/2437